PRIMARY SOURCES OF
FAMOUS PEOPLE IN AMERICAN HISTORY™

CRISPUS ATTUCKS

HERO OF THE BOSTON MASSACRE
HÉROE DE LA MASACRE DE BOSTON

ANNE BEIER

TRADUCCIÓN AL ESPAÑOL:
TOMÁS GONZÁLEZ

rosen central
Primary Source™
Editorial Buenas Letras™

The Rosen Publishing Group, Inc., New York

To Christopher W. Douglass, and in memory of Warner Feig

Published in 2004 by The Rosen Publishing Group, Inc.
29 East 21st Street, New York, NY 10010

First Bilingual Edition 2004
First English Edition 2004

Cataloging Data

Beier, Anne.
[Crispus Attucks. Bilingual]
Crispus Attucks / by Anne Beier; translation into Spanish, Tomás González
     p. cm. — (Primary Sources of famous people in American history)
Summary: Introduces the life of Crispus Attucks, a former slave who died in the Boston Massacre, a fight between the British and American colonists that occurred before the American Revolution.
Includes bibliographical references and index.
ISBN 0-8239-4154-X (library binding)
1. Attucks, Crispus, d. 1770—Juvenile literature. 2. Boston Massacre, 1770—Juvenile literature. 3. African Americans—Biography—Juvenile literature. [1. Attucks, Crispus, d. 1770. 2. Boston Massacre, 1770. 3. African Americans—Biography. 3. Spanish Language Materials—Bilingual.]
I. Title. II. Series: Primary sources of famous people in American history.
E185.97.A86 B45 2003
973.3'113'092—dc21

Manufactured in the United States of America

Photo credits: cover, pp. 5, 21, 23, 29 © Hulton/Archive/Getty Images; p. 7 The New-York Historical Society, New York, USA/The Bridgeman Art Library; p. 9 Christie's Images/The Bridgeman Art Library; pp. 11, 25 © North Wind Picture Archives; p. 13 Yale University Art Gallery, New Haven, CT/The Bridgeman Art Library; pp. 15, 27 Picture Collection, The Branch Libraries, The New York Public Library, Astor, Lenox, and Tilden Foundations; p. 17 Archives Charmet/The Bridgeman Art Library; p. 19 Bonhams, London, UK/The Bridgeman Art Library.

Designer: Thomas Forget; Photo Researcher: Rebecca Anguin-Cohen

CONTENTS

CONTENIDO

1 A YOUNG LAD WITH BIG DREAMS

In 1723, Crispus Attucks was born into slavery in Framingham, Massachusetts. His father, Prince, was captured in Africa. He was brought to the colonies and sold as a slave. Nancy, Crispus's mother, was a member of the Natick Indian tribe. Crispus had an older sister, Phebe. The family served their master, Colonel Buckminster.

---

1 UN JOVEN CON GRANDES SUEÑOS

En 1723, Crispus Attucks nació en la esclavitud en Framingham, Massachusetts. Su padre, Prince, fue capturado en África, traído a las colonias y vendido como esclavo. Nancy, madre de Crispus, pertenecía a la tribu de indios Natick. Crispus tenía una hermana mayor, Phebe. La familia servía a su amo, el coronel Buckminster.

This drawing of Crispus Attucks is one of the few that exist.

Este es uno de los pocos dibujos que existen de Crispus Attucks.

In his early teens, Crispus wanted to be free. He did not like the idea of being owned. Attucks dreamed of becoming a sailor. Colonel Buckminster had no ships. Later, Attucks was sold to a new master, William Brown. Crispus was forced to move to Boston near the shipping docks.

Crispus quería ser libre desde que tenía unos diez años. No le gustaba la idea de ser propiedad de alguien. Attucks soñaba con ser marino, pero el coronel Buckminster no tenía barcos. Más tarde, Attucks fue vendido a un nuevo amo, William Brown, y obligado a trasladarse a Boston, cerca de los muelles.

Boston Harbor around 1800. Ships from Europe sailed into the harbor every week.

La bahía de Boston en 1800, aproximadamente. Cada semana llegaban barcos procedentes de Europa.

William Brown taught Crispus the cattle business. He bought and sold cattle for his master. Crispus became very good at his new trade. His dreams of becoming a free man had not died. Attucks did not like that dark-skinned people were forced into slavery. He wanted to escape slavery and become a sailor.

William Brown enseñó a Crispus el negocio del ganado. Crispus compraba y vendía ganado para su amo. Se volvió muy eficiente en su nuevo oficio, pero sus sueños de ser hombre libre no habían disminuido. A Attucks no le gustaba que se esclavizara a la gente de piel oscura. Quería escapar de la esclavitud y convertirse en marino.

Crispus Attucks kept extra money he made from selling cows.

Crispus Attucks ahorraba el dinero extra que obtenía al vender ganado.

2 ATTUCKS MAKES A PLAN

Crispus watched the ships that always returned to the harbor. Soon he was able to spot a stray ship. It was a whaling ship. One night William Brown was away. Crispus slipped away to talk to the captain. The captain liked that Crispus was a big, strong man. Crispus was also known to be tough and a fighter.

---

2 ATTUCKS TIENE UN PLAN

Crispus observaba a los barcos en la bahía. Muy pronto descubrió un barco que se había desviado de su ruta. Era un barco ballenero. Una noche en que William Brown no estaba en casa, Crispus se escabulló para hablar con el capitán. Al capitán le agradó que Crispus fuera grande y fuerte. Además Crispus tenía fama de rudo y luchador.

Whaling ships captured whales for their blubber (fat).

Los barcos balleneros cazaban ballenas para extraerles la grasa.

The captain hired him that night. Crispus went below deck to hide. He worried that he might be captured before the ship left port. The ship sailed out to sea the next morning. Crispus was happy that his dreams were coming true.

El capitán lo contrató esa misma noche. Crispus se ocultó bajo cubierta. Le preocupaba ser capturado antes de que el barco dejara el puerto. A la mañana siguiente el barco navegó mar adentro. Crispus se sintió feliz de que su sueño se estuviera haciendo realidad.

Whaling sailors did not use the ship to capture whales. A group of men set out in a large rowboat.

Los balleneros no cazaban las ballenas desde el barco. El grupo de cazadores salía en una lancha grande de remos.

Soon after, William Brown discovered that Crispus had run away. On October 2, 1750, Brown placed an announcement in the *Boston Gazette*. It stated that Crispus Attucks was a runaway slave. From then on, Crispus always had to be careful. If he was caught, he would lose his newfound freedom.

Poco después, William Brown descubrió que Crispus había escapado. El 2 de octubre de 1750, puso un aviso en el periódico *Boston Gazette*. En el se decía que Crispus Attucks era un esclavo fugitivo. Desde ese día Crispus tuvo que ser muy cuidadoso. Si lo atrapaban perdería la libertad recién ganada.

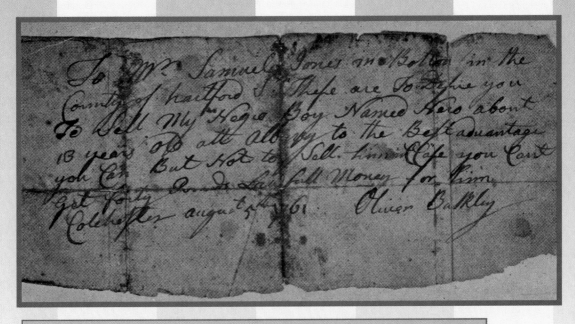

This bill of sale shows how easily slave families could be broken apart.

Esta factura muestra lo sencillo que era separar a una familia de esclavos.

3 TWENTY YEARS AT SEA

For the next twenty years, Crispus worked on ships at sea. He learned to hunt and catch whales. Work on whaling ships was dangerous.

Crispus learned to throw a harpoon. In those days, whales were worth a lot of money. Whale blubber was turned into oil for burning in lamps.

3 VEINTE AÑOS EN EL MAR

Durante los veinte años siguientes Crispus trabajó en barcos en el mar. Aprendió a cazar ballenas. Trabajar en los barcos balleneros era peligroso.

Crispus aprendió a lanzar el arpón. En aquellos días las ballenas valían mucho dinero. La grasa de las ballenas era convertida en aceite para encender lámparas.

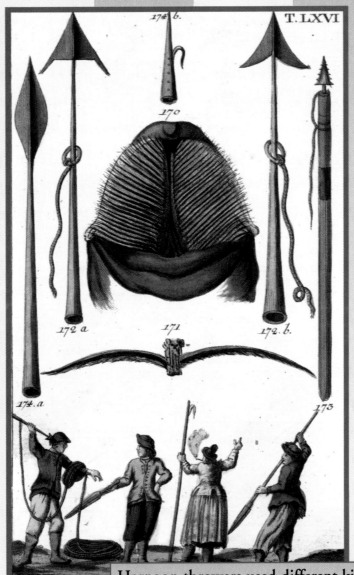

Harpoon throwers used different kinds of tips.

Los arponeros utilizaban diferentes clases de puntas.

17

Whaling captains valued Crispus's hard work and courage. As a harpooner, he earned good wages. Crispus missed his family, though. He was at sea most of the year. Sometimes the ship returned to Boston. At these times, Crispus secretly visited his family. Luckily, he was never caught.

Los capitanes de los barcos balleneros apreciaban la diligencia y la valentía de Crispus. Como arponero ganaba un buen salario. Sin embargo, permanecía en el mar la mayor parte del año y extrañaba a su familia. A veces el barco iba a Boston y entonces Crispus visitaba en secreto a su familia. Por fortuna, nunca fue atrapado.

Whaling was a hard job. Sometimes the whale would overturn the boat.

Cazar ballenas era un trabajo duro. A veces, las ballenas hacían zozobrar las embarcaciones.

4 TOUGH TIMES FOR THE AMERICAN COLONIES

In the 1770s, American colonists wanted independence from Great Britain. King George of England did not like this idea. He sent British soldiers to control the colonists. King George placed high taxes on goods sent to the colonies. This angered the colonists. Life became uneasy between the British and the colonists.

---

4 TIEMPOS DIFÍCILES PARA LAS COLONIAS

En la década de 1770, los colonos querían independizarse de Gran Bretaña. Al rey Jorge de Inglaterra no le gustaba la idea y envió soldados británicos para que controlaran a los colonos. El rey gravó con impuestos altos los bienes de consumo que se enviaban a las colonias, lo cual enojó a los colonos. Las relaciones entre ambos se hicieron difíciles.

People in all the colonies spoke out against high taxes. Colonists began to fight for freedom.

En todas las colonias la gente protestó los altos impuestos. Los colonos comenzaron a luchar por la libertad.

Crispus continued to work on whalers during the 1770s. He often heard about the trouble in the colonies. He understood their strong need for independence. He had been working and hiding for his own freedom. Crispus wanted to help the colonists' cause. He feared being captured and returned to slavery, though.

———•◆•———

Durante la década de 1770, Crispus siguió trabajando en los barcos balleneros. A menudo escuchaba noticias sobre los problemas que se estaban presentando en las colonias. Entendía su fuerte necesidad de independencia, pues él mismo había tenido que esconderse y luchar por su libertad. Crispus quería ayudar a la causa de los colonos. Sin embargo, temía que lo capturaran y volvieran a hacerlo esclavo.

Colonial political leaders began to meet in each colony.
They decided to unite in their cause.

Los líderes de las colonias comenzaron a reunirse. Los líderes
decidieron unirse para luchar por su causa.

5 THE BOSTON MASSACRE

On the evening of March 5, 1770, Crispus was in Boston. A colonist had done some work for a British soldier that night. The soldier refused to pay him. Quickly, news spread through Boston of this injustice. Colonists gathered in the streets. They yelled and threw snowballs and rocks at the British soldiers. The soldiers fought back.

---

5 LA MASACRE DE BOSTON

La noche del 5 de marzo de 1770, Crispus estaba en Boston. Esa noche un colono le había hecho un trabajo a un soldado británico y el soldado rehusó pagarle. Muy pronto se corrió la voz de esta injusticia por todo Boston. Los colonos se reunieron en las calles. Gritaban a los soldados británicos y les lanzaban bolas de nieve y piedras. Los soldados respondieron.

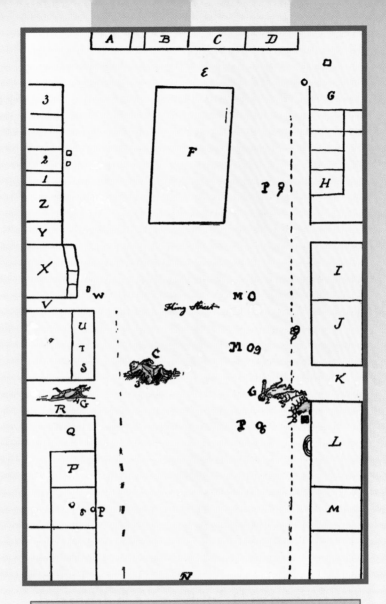

Paul Revere drew this map of the Boston Massacre site. He used letters and numbers to place people.

Paul Revere dibujó este mapa de la Masacre de Boston. Utilizó números y letras para situar a la gente.

The soldiers hit colonists with sticks and the tips of their muskets. Crispus bravely joined his fellow colonists. He did not care about the color of their skin. The fight for freedom was more important to him. A big fight broke out on King Street in front of the Customs House. Crispus tried to grab a musket from one of the soldiers.

Los soldados golpearon a los colonos con palos y con sus mosquetes. Crispus se unió a los colonos. No le importaba de qué color tenían la piel. Para él era más importante la lucha por la libertad. En la calle King, al frente del Edificio de las Aduanas, estalló una gran pelea. Crispus trató de arrebatarle el mosquete a uno de los soldados.

Another drawing of the Boston Massacre shows a larger crowd. Crispus Attucks was one of the first to die.

Otro dibujo de la Masacre de Boston muestra una multitud aún más grande. Crispus Attucks fue uno de los primeros en morir.

A British soldier shot and killed Crispus. Four other colonists were killed that night. Crispus Attucks was one of the first people to give his life for American independence. The Boston Massacre led to the Revolutionary War. The colonists won the war and became independent from Britain's rule. Crispus gave his life to help free the very colonists who once enslaved him.

———◆———

Un soldado británico le disparó a Crispus y lo mató. Esa noche murieron otros cuatro colonos. Crispus Attucks fue una de las primeras personas en dar la vida por la independencia de Estados Unidos. La Masacre de Boston llevó a la Guerra de Independencia. Los colonos ganaron la guerra y se independizaron de los británicos. Crispus dio la vida por la libertad de los mismos colonos que una vez lo esclavizaron.

Hours to the Gates of this City many Thousands of our brave Brethren in the Country, deeply affected with our Distresses, and to whom we are greatly obliged on this Occasion—No one knows where this would have ended, and what important Consequences even to the whole British Empire might have followed, which our Moderation & Loyalty upon so trying an Occasion, and our Faith in the Commander's Assurances have happily prevented.

Last Thursday, agreeable to a general Request of the Inhabitants, and by the Consent of Parents and Friends, were carried to their *Grave* in Succession, the Bodies of *Samuel Gray, Samuel Maverick, James Caldwell*, and *Crispus Attucks*, the unhappy Victims who fell in the bloody Massacre of the Monday Evening preceeding!

On this Occasion most of the Shops in Town were shut, all the Bells were ordered to toll a solemn Peal, as were also those in the neighboring Towns of Charlestown Roxbury, &c. The Procession began to move between the Hours of 4 and 5 in the Afternoon ; two of the unfortunate Sufferers, viz. Mess. *James Caldwell* and *Crispus Attucks*, who were Strangers, borne from Faneuil-Hall,

Colonial newspapers wrote about the five dead men from the Boston Massacre.

Los periódicos coloniales escribieron sobre las cinco víctimas de la Masacre de Boston.

TIMELINE

1723—Crispus and his family are slaves in Framingham, Massachusetts.

1750—Crispus runs away to become a sailor.

1750-1770—Crispus works on a whaling ship.

1770—Crispus is one of the first men killed in the fight for American independence. This event became known as the Boston Massacre.

CRONOLOGÍA

1723—Nace Crispus Attucks. Él y su familia son esclavos y viven en Framingham, Massachusetts.

1750—Crispus escapa para convertirse en marino.

1750-1770—Crispus trabaja en un barco ballenero.

1770—Crispus fue uno de las primeros muertos en la lucha por la independencia de Estados Unidos. Murió en un evento conocido como la Masacre de Boston.

GLOSSARY

announcement (uh-NOUNSS-ment) Something that is stated officially or publicly.

courage (KUR-ij) Bravery or fearlessness.

freedom (FREE-duhm) The right to do and say what one wants.

injustice (in-JUHSS-tiss) An unfair act.

musket (MUHSS-kit) A gun with a long barrel that was used before the rifle was invented.

slavery (SLAYV-re) When someone is owned by another person and thought of as property.

WEB SITES

GLOSARIO

anuncio (el) Algo que se avisa oficial o públicamente.

esclavitud (la) Cuando una persona es dominada por otra persona que la considera su propiedad.

injusticia (la) Acto arbitrario o injusto.

libertad (la) Derecho a hacer o decir lo que se quiere.

mosquete (el) Arma de fuego de cañón largo que se utilizó antes de la invención del rifle.

valentía Valor o ausencia de miedo.

SITIOS WEB

INDEX

ABOUT THE AUTHOR

Anne Beier writes children's books, and teaches creative writing and art for children at the NWCA. Anne lives with her husband and cat in Ossining, New York.

ÍNDICE

ACERCA DEL AUTOR

Anne Beier escribe libros para niños y enseña escritura creativa y arte a los niños en la asociación NWCA. Anne vive con su esposo y su gato en Ossining, Nueva York.